SOLO TENOR or ALTO SAXOPHONE
or other B♭/E♭ Instrument

T0087400

Too Marvelous
for
Words

STANDARDS FOR SAXOPHONE

VOLUME 1

PLAYBACK+
Speed • Pitch • Balance • Loop

To access audio visit:
www.halleonard.com/mylibrary

Enter Code
2633-4234-7402-7712

ISBN 978-1-59615-837-5

MMO Music Minus One

EXCLUSIVELY DISTRIBUTED BY

HAL•LEONARD®

Visit Hal Leonard Online at
www.halleonard.com

Contact Us:
Hal Leonard
7777 West Bluemound Road
Milwaukee, WI 53213
Email: info@halleonard.com

In Europe contact:
Hal Leonard Europe Limited
Distribution Centre, Newmarket Road
Bury St Edmunds, Suffolk, IP33 3YB
Email: info@halleonardeurope.com

In Australia contact:
Hal Leonard Australia Pty. Ltd.
4 Lentara Court
Cheltenham, Victoria, 3192 Australia
Email: info@halleonard.com.au

In his career, **Glenn Zottola** has been best known as a brilliant and swinging trumpeter who occasionally doubled quite effectively on alto. But on this special project, he is heard as a talented tenor-saxophonist who draws on the sounds and styles of Lester Young and Coleman Hawkins, finding his own voice somewhere in between. Glenn sounds quite at home playing with the vintage rhythm sections, yet gives the music his own twist and never tries to just merely copy or recreate the past.

Relatively few jazz musicians have been equally comfortable on both brass and reed instruments. Benny Carter, Ira Sullivan and Scott Robinson come to mind along with just a handful of others. Glenn was never told that it was difficult to play both brass and reeds, so he developed his own musical conceptions, giving one the impression that it is effortless. But that is consistent with his career, for he has often made the difficult seem natural.

Glenn Zottola was born and raised in Port Chester, New York. His father Frank Zottola played trumpet, was an important arranger for Claude Thornhill's orchestra, and became the maker of trumpet mouthpieces while Glenn's brother Bob Zottola (who is ten years older) also plays trumpet. Glenn followed in the family tradition, starting on the trumpet when he was just three. While his father was an inspiring figure, his mother played piano in a style similar to Count Basie, taught Glenn hundreds of standards, and often jammed with him. By the time he was seven, Glenn made his debut playing before his second grade class. With that fast start, Glenn was considered a bit of a child prodigy. He won the Ted Mack Amateur Show three times and toured with the Ted Mack Show for a year. He appeared on television in a variety of settings including The Chubby Jackson Show, led a band with Chubby's son drummer Duffy Jackson when he was a teenager, and toured with cornetist Bobby Hackett and trombonist Jack Teagarden when he was still just 11.

Glenn picked up very valuable training a few years later. His parents had a jazz club, brother Bob headed the house band (which included such notables as Tommy Flanagan, Sonny Clark, Bobby Timmons or Ray Bryant on piano and Bobby Jaspar or Booker Ervin on tenor), and the young trumpeter performed each week with the all-star group. Even that early on, it was never a matter of him being considered a novelty due to his youth; he held his own with such fast company. When he was 13, Glenn began doubling on tenor sax, soon switching to alto. Other than one lesson to learn the fingerings, he was completely self taught, finding it surprisingly easy and fun to alternate between his horns.

In the 1970s, Glenn Zottola emerged on the national jazz scene. He had stints with the Glenn Miller Orchestra (during a period when clarinetist Buddy DeFranco led the band) and toured with Lionel Hampton. He worked in the pits of Broadway musicals, gigged with Mel Torme and Tex Beneke and really gained strong notice as a member of the Benny Goodman Sextet during 1977-79. One of the early "Young Lions" who emerged at the time who invigorated creative swing, Glenn got along well with Goodman who admired his obvious musical talent.

After the Goodman period, Glenn led a modern mainstream quartet that included pianist Harold Danko and drummer Butch Miles. Next up was an important association with Bob Wilber's Bechet Legacy where he shared the frontline with Wilber, had opportunities to play classic jazz and hot swing, and returned to his roots in Louis Armstrong. The tours and recordings of Bechet Legacy gave Glenn high visibility in the jazz world. After leaving Wilber, Glenn teamed up with pianist Mark Shane and a drummer to form the Classic Jazz Trio. They toured England and recorded *Jazz Titans* (Classic Jazz 2), an outstanding showcase (released for the first time in 2011) that features Glenn in top form.

Back in the United States, Glenn Zottola's career took a very surprising turn. He sat in with actress-singer Suzanne Somers, melted her heart with his rendition of "But Beautiful," and was hired as her bandleader. For nine years he performed with Somers for her Las Vegas shows, tours, appearances, and finally her daytime television show. While this resulted in him spending years away from the jazz world, Glenn performed before literally tens of millions of viewers, interacted with guest celebrities, and even for a time had a big office next door to Steven Spielberg. It was quite a difference from being on the typical jazz tour, and the first-class treatment was well deserved.

Since the "Suzanne Somers Show" ended in 1995, Glenn Zottola has been musically active but on his own terms. He made recordings with Steve Allen and drummer Hugh Barlow and has also recorded privately for several thus far unreleased projects. He has often played with his friend Chick Corea, challenging himself in his explorations of modern jazz while never being shy to display his roots in classic jazz. Glenn has also been working with Beverly Getz (Stan's daughter) in plans to introduce jazz to kids in schools.

Another special project is this recording. Although he has loved playing tenor since he picked up his first saxophone when he was 13, Glenn Zottola had never recorded a full set on that instrument. Making this recording even more unique is that Glenn is heard playing along with some of the earliest performances recorded for the acclaimed Music Minus One series. Dating from 1952, the rhythm sections feature such notables as pianists Nat Pierce and Don Abney, and guitarists Mundell Lowe and Jimmy Raney taking short solos while bassist Milt Hinton, Oscar Pettiford and Wilbur Ware, and drummers Osie Johnson, Kenny Clarke and Bobby Donaldson give quiet and steady support. Because Glenn has a timeless and very flexible style, he adapts his playing on this unique set, sounding a bit like a cousin of Lester Young and Stan Getz. His style, hinting at swing, bop and cool jazz, fits the era perfectly.

Performing 10 standards including "Too Marvelous For Words," "Body And Soul," "Three Little Words" and "Fine And Dandy," Glenn Zottola plays creatively within the style of 1952 cool swing without sacrificing his own individuality. If given a blindfold test, few listeners would guess that Glenn's playing took place nearly 60 years after that of the rhythm sections, and some might speculate that this was a long lost session recorded at the Lighthouse.

In any case, this is timeless music and quite fun to hear.

Scott Yanow, author of ten books including *Swing*, *Bebop*, *Trumpet Kings*, *Jazz On Film* and *Jazz On Record 1917-76*

My thanks to my friend Les Silver of RS Berkeley Instruments for providing me with the Virtuoso Vintage Tenor and Stan Getz Legend Mouthpiece which I used on this album, both truly a joy to work with. Thanks also to Robert Polan and Kristen McKeon of Rico Reeds for allowing me to test literally dozens of reeds before recording. As any saxophone player will tell you, without a good reed all is for naught.
Glenn Zottola

CONTENTS

FOREWORD

THIS ALBUM is actually the culmination of something that started a long time ago. When I was 13 years old, I was endorsing trumpets for the Leblanc Corporation. At that time, having a love for the tenor sax, I asked Vito Pascucci (the president of the company) if he would send me a Tenor Saxophone to try, which he did. I took one lesson to learn the fingerings and then went off on my own. I drifted off to the alto, which was lighter to hold and higher in pitch—closer to the trumpet—and never had time in my busy career to fulfill what I heard in my head and loved regarding the tenor. With the help of Irv Kratka at MMO, I have now, 50 years later—after an illustrious career that I wouldn't trade for anything—fulfilled that dream, for which I am very thankful. Let me say something about these wonderful tracks that I used for this album from the first and historic MMO recordings of 1952. Being primarily an "ear player," I didn't enjoy practicing out of a book when I was a kid, and simply wanted to play the music I already heard in my head right away. These early MMO albums allowed me the freedom to do that and contributed greatly to my being able to shape my own sound and style as a jazz artist. Little did I know later in my life I would get the privilege to play, record and become friends with some of the jazz legends on this original MMO record. Let me say something also about the music on this album. I approached this album like I was putting together a set to play at a jazz club on 52nd street in NYC during the golden age of jazz, when you could walk down that street on any given night and hear tenor players like Coleman Hawkins, Lester Young, Stan Getz and many more playing in clubs. I wanted to incorporate all the "nuances" that I love about this style of jazz that I learned from being mentored by the greats from an early age, with sound, feel, expression, dynamics and "relaxed groove" being paramount. This rhythm section provides a canvas to do that without equal. My basic advice to the student is: When you play, try to tell a story, make it swing and create beauty!

I would like to first thank my mom and dad, both wonderful musicians, for providing me the environment to pursue music. My mom would sit me on her knee when I was three years old and play the piano (she played like Count Basie) teaching me hundreds of beautiful standards, like the ones on this album, that are the very fabric of my musical soul. My dad, beside being my first trumpet teacher, would sit at my bedside and put on beautiful melodic operatic music, and Debussy—as he was a conductor—and make up stories to the music to put me asleep instead of reading from a normal children's book. I would like to thank my wife Diana of 32 years for the continual and ongoing support, which has been a constant source of stability both in life and career.

I also would like to thank my friend Les Silver of RS Berkeley Instruments for providing me with the Virtuoso Vintage Tenor and Stan Getz legend mouthpiece I used on this album, both truly a joy to play; along with Robert Polan and Kristen Mckeon of Rico Reeds for providing the reeds used on this recording. As any saxophone player will tell you, without a good reed all is for naught.

I haven't recorded by choice since my TV show closed, and I would like to thank my dear friend and jazz great Chick Corea, who is always an inspiration for all the encouragement, along with Beverly Getz for carrying forward the legacy of her dad who was one of the inspirations for this album, and last but not least, my dear friend and master teacher Herk Faranda, who gave me so much support preparing for this project.

I would like to dedicate this album to my beautiful new grandchild, Waverly, who is definitely "Too Marvelous For Words" and came into the world during the recording of this album—certainly a good omen!

Enjoy !

—*Glenn Zottola - December 2011*

SOLO B♭ TENOR SAXOPHONE
or E♭ ALTO SAXOPHONE

Too Marvelous For Words

Words by JOHNNY MERCER
Music by RICHARD A. WHITING

MMO 12221

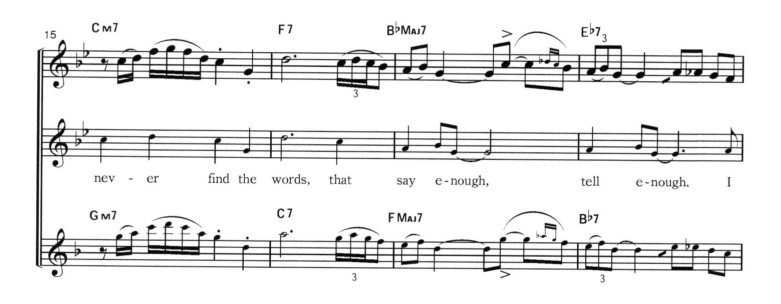

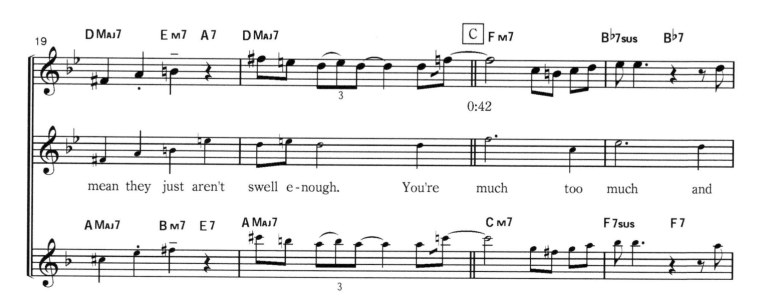

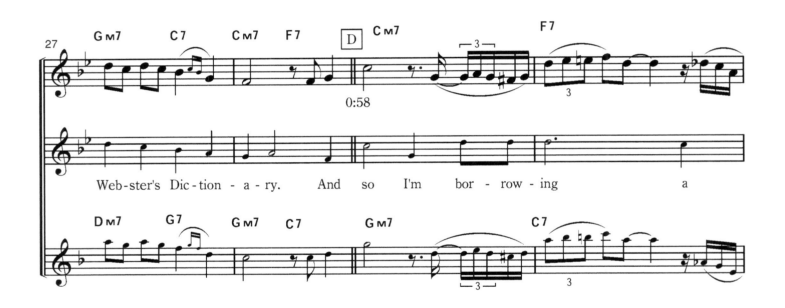

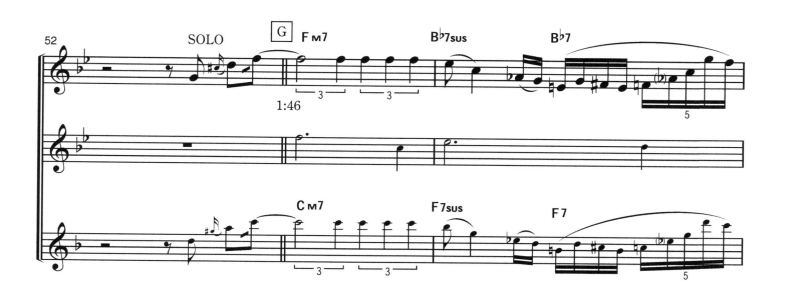

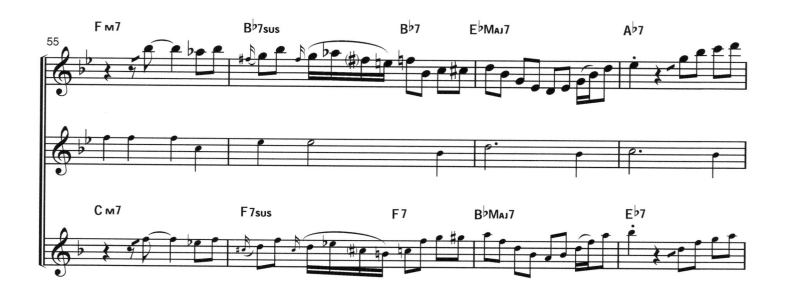

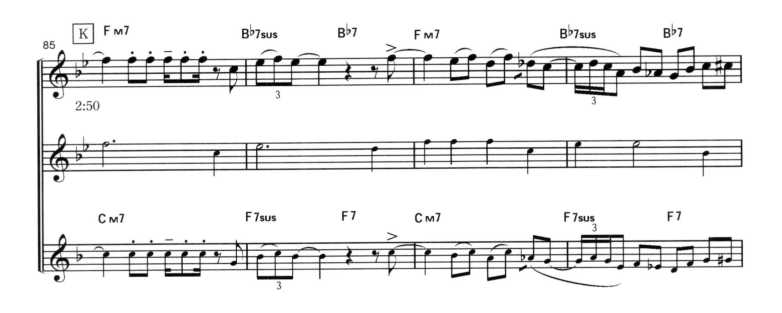

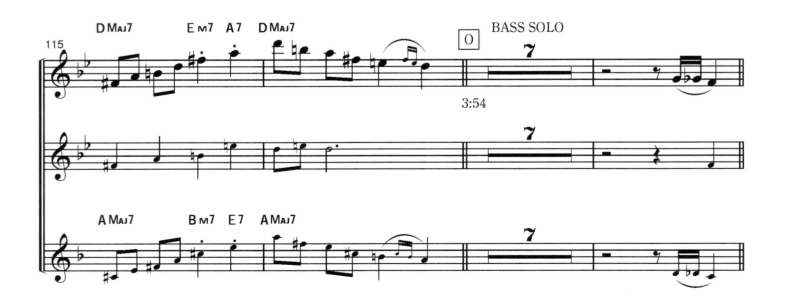

SOLO B♭ TENOR SAXOPHONE
or E♭ ALTO SAXOPHONE

Body And Soul

Words by EDWARD HEYMAN, ROBERT SOUR
and FRANK EYTON
Music by JOHN GREEN

I'll glad - ly sur - ren - - - der

my - self to you bo - dy and soul.

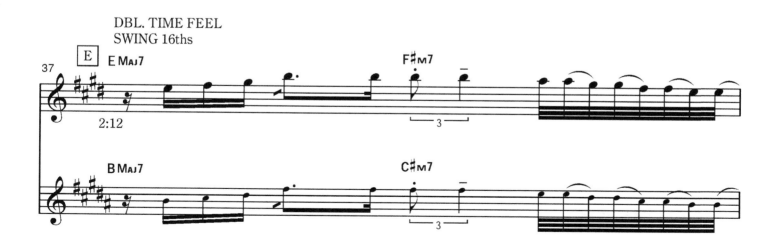

DBL. TIME FEEL
SWING 16ths

2:12

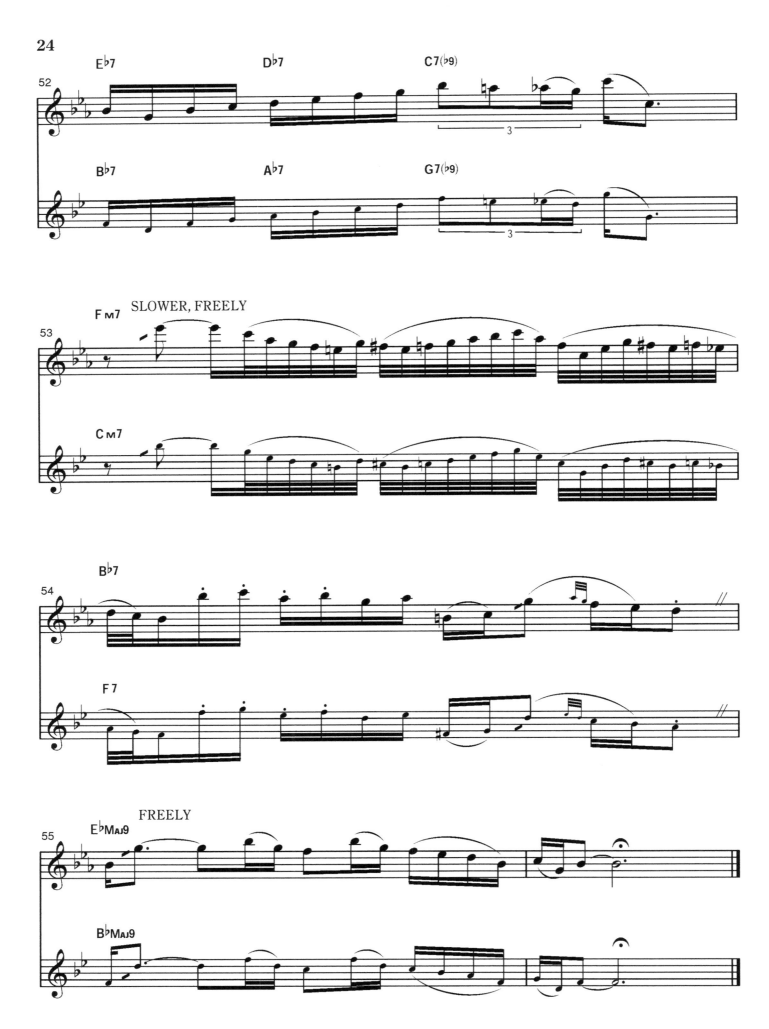

SOLO B♭ TENOR SAXOPHONE
or E♭ ALTO SAXOPHONE

Oh, Lady Be Good!

Music and Lyrics by
GEORGE GERSHWIN and IRA GERSHWIN

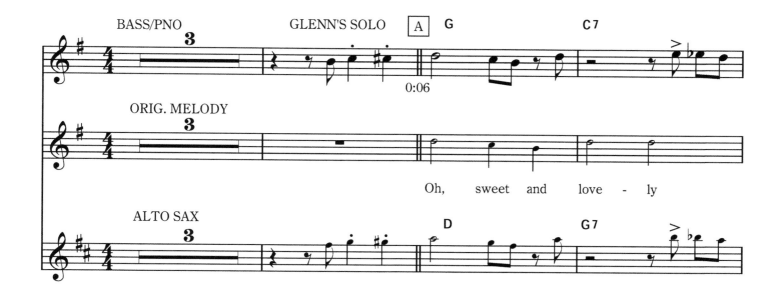

MMO 12221

32

MMO 12221

SOLO B♭ TENOR SAXOPHONE
or E♭ ALTO SAXOPHONE

Embraceable You

Music and Lyrics by
GEORGE GERSHWIN and IRA GERSHWIN

come to pa - pa, come to pa - pa, do.

My sweet em - brace - - a - ble

you.

SOLO Bb TENOR SAXOPHONE
or Eb ALTO SAXOPHONE

Three Little Words
from the Motion Picture CHECK AND DOUBLE CHECK

Lyric by Bert Kalmar
Music by Harry Ruby

44

MMO 12221

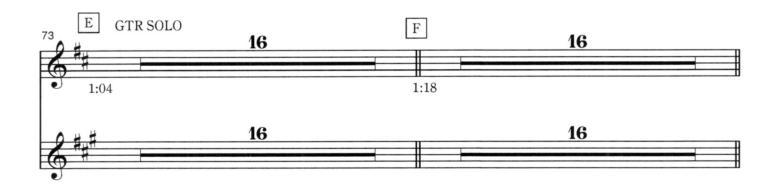

47

MMO 12221

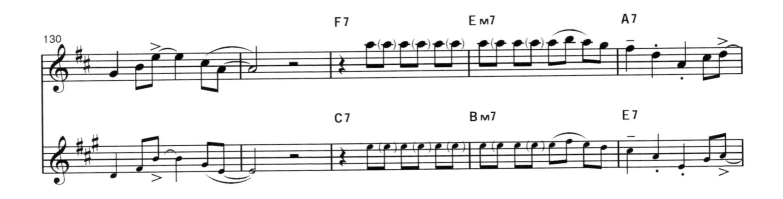

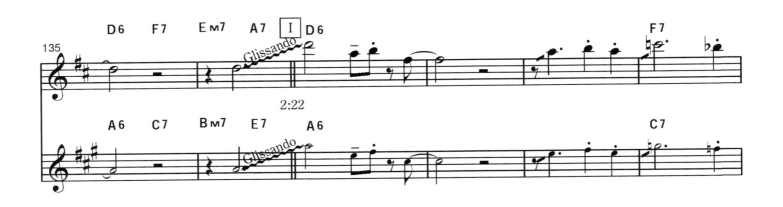

SOLO B♭ TENOR SAXOPHONE
or E♭ ALTO SAXOPHONE

Poor Butterfly

Words by JOHN L. GOLDEN
Music by RAYMOND HUBBELL

54

SOLO B♭ TENOR SAXOPHONE
or E♭ ALTO SAXOPHONE

Sometimes I'm Happy

Words by IRVING CAESAR and CLIFFORD GREY
Music by VINCENT YOUMANS

MMO 12221

66

SOLO B♭ TENOR SAXOPHONE
or E♭ ALTO SAXOPHONE

You Go To My Head

Words by HAVEN GILLESPIE
Music by J. FRED COOTS

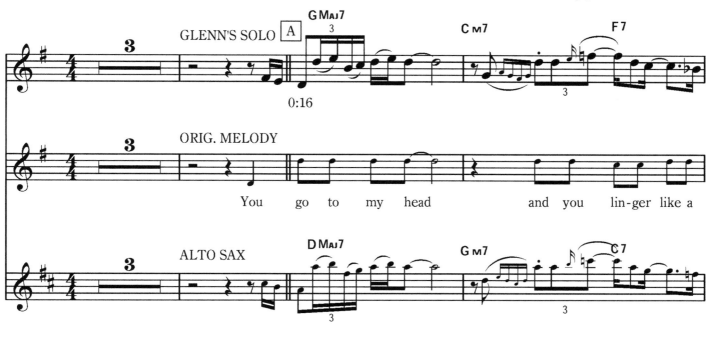

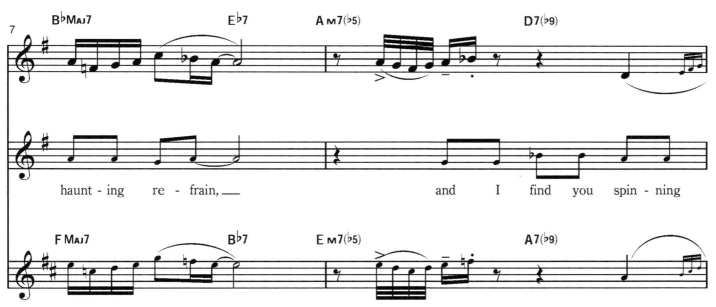

MMO 12221

men-tion of you like the kick-er in a ju-lep or two.

The thrill of the thought that you

might give a thoughto my plea casts a spell o - ver me. Still I

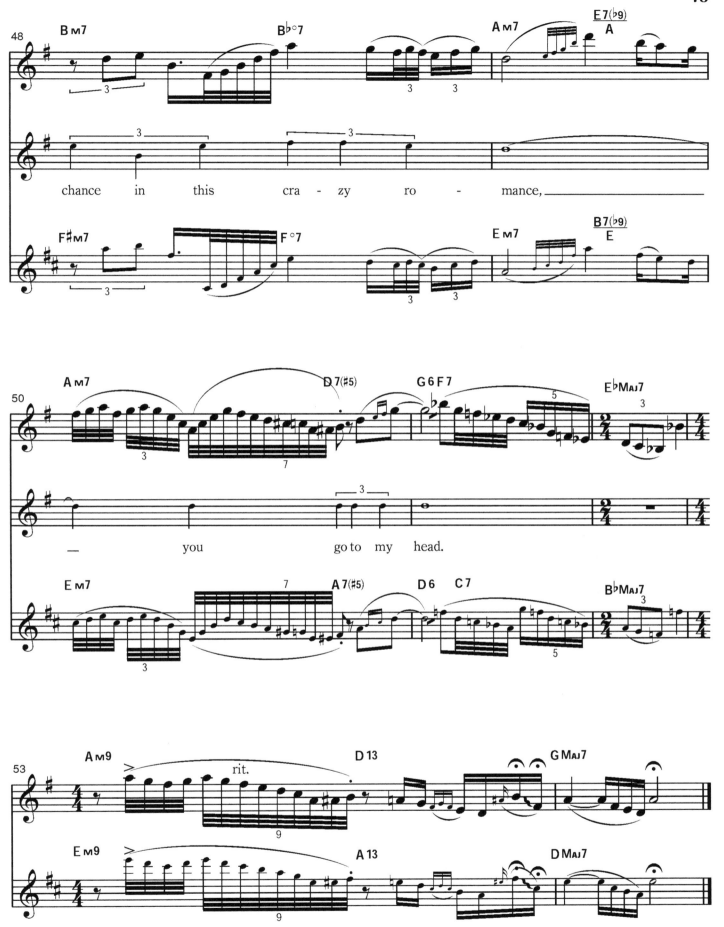

chance in this cra - zy ro - mance,_____

_____ you go to my head.

SOLO Bb TENOR SAXOPHONE
or Eb ALTO SAXOPHONE

When Your Lover Has Gone

Words and Music by
E.A. SWAN

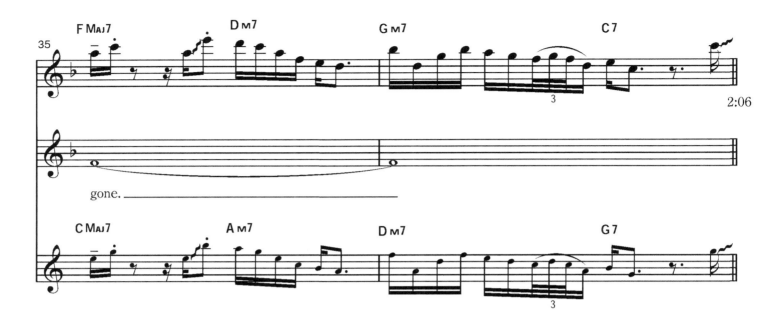

2:06

gone.

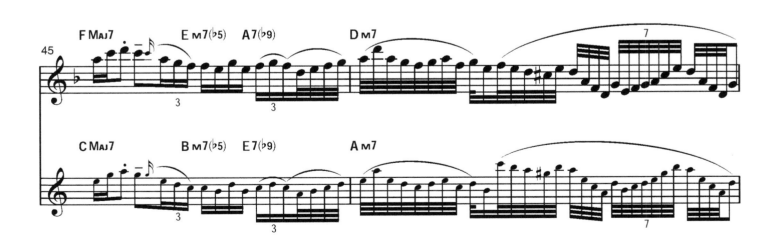

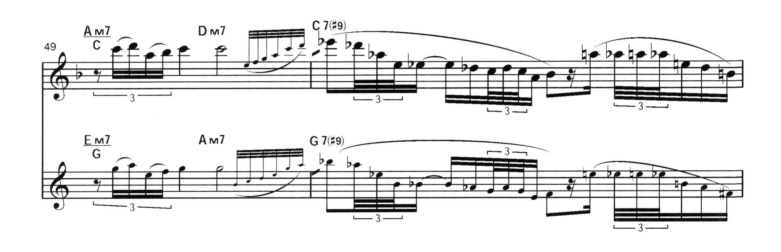

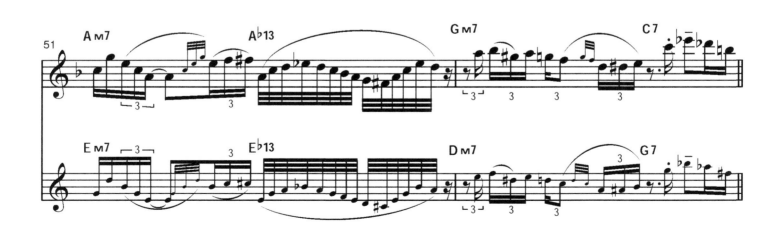

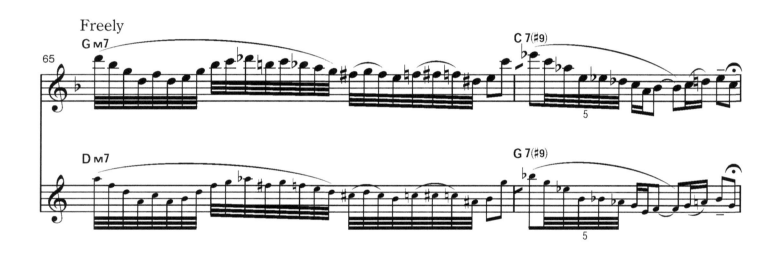

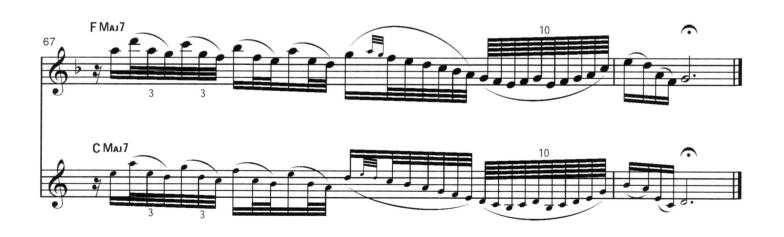

SOLO B♭ TENOR SAXOPHONE
or E♭ ALTO SAXOPHONE

Fine and Dandy

Words and Music by
KAY SWIFT and PAUL JAMES

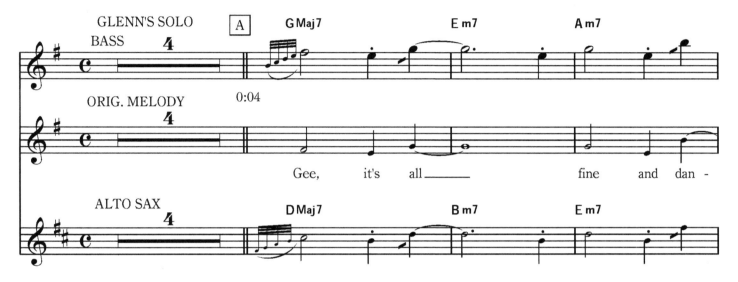

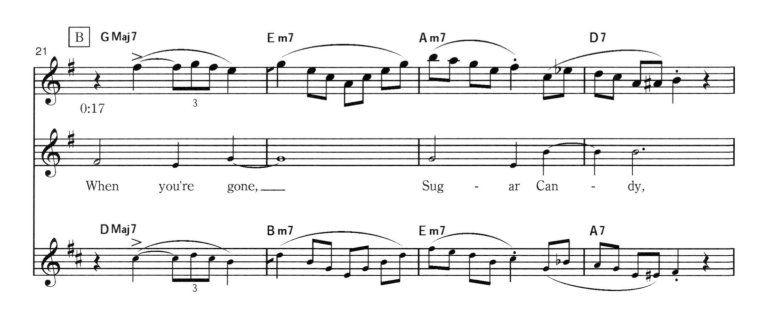

88

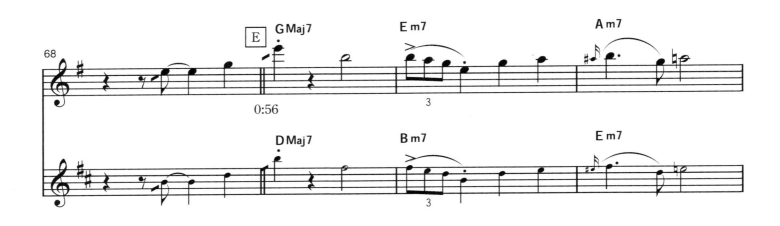

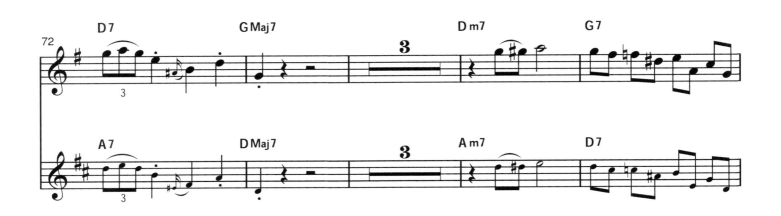

Transcription and Engraving by Joel Mott
jtldmott@comcast.net

MMO 12221

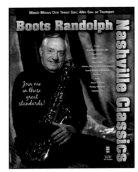

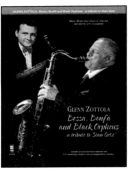

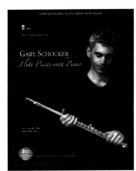